My Uncle's Factory Produces Solar Panels

Lamar Coldwell

I0809689

Rosen REAL READERS

Rosen Classroom™
New York

This is my uncle Ray. He owns a **factory**. The factory produces **solar panels**.

Solar energy comes from the sun. Sun rays produce heat. Sun rays can also be used to generate electricity.

Solar panels absorb sun rays and make electricity. These solar panels are on a roof.

Solar panels for homes are made at the factory. They are placed on top of homes.

Some solar panels produce electricity at **power plants**. They are made at the factory. These panels are larger than the ones made for homes. They are more expensive, too.

Solar panels are made by many people. **Engineers** design solar panels. They draw up plans. They also make models of solar panels.

Some people buy solar panels for their homes. They order them from the factory. This woman works at the factory. She takes a call from a family who orders solar panels for their home.

The solar panels are made in the factory. Then they are brought to the family's house. Workmen place the solar panels on the roof.

Workmen install solar panels. They use tools to secure them to the roof. This worker is using a screwdriver. He attaches the solar panel to the roof.

The solar panels are ready to use. They absorb sunlight. The solar panels make electricity that heats the family's home.

Glossary

engineer A person who designs and builds machines or equipment.

factory A building where goods are made and assembled.

power plant A building where electricity is produced for a large area.

solar panel A panel that absorbs sunlight and produces energy.